Scuba Diving

Tom Greve

ROURKE PUBLISHING
Vero Beach, Florida 32964

www.rourkepublishing.com

PHOTO CREDITS: © Durden Images: cover; © Annetje: title page; © Cornelis Opstal: pages 2-3; © frantisekhojdysz: page 5; © Wolfgang Amri: page 6; © Sergiy Zavgorodny: page 7; © Associated Press: page 8; © Jason Maehl: page 10; © Fukuoka Irina: page 11; © Wolfgang Steiner: page 12; © Elisei Shafer: page 13; © oksana.perkins: page 15; © Dropu: pages 16-17; © RCB Shooter: pages 18-19; © Rich Carey: pages 21, 22

Edited by Jeanne Sturm

Cover designed by Tara Raymo
Interior designed by Heather Botto

Library of Congress Cataloging-in-Publication Data

Greve, Tom.
  Scuba diving / Tom Greve.
      p. cm. -- (Action sports)
  Includes index.
  ISBN 978-1-60694-364-9
  1. Scuba diving--Juvenile literature. I. Title.
  GV838.672.G75 2009
  797.2'3--dc22

                          2009006063

Printed in the USA

CG/CG

ROURKE PUBLISHING

www.rourkepublishing.com - rourke@rourkepublishing.com
Post Office Box 643328 Vero Beach, Florida 32964

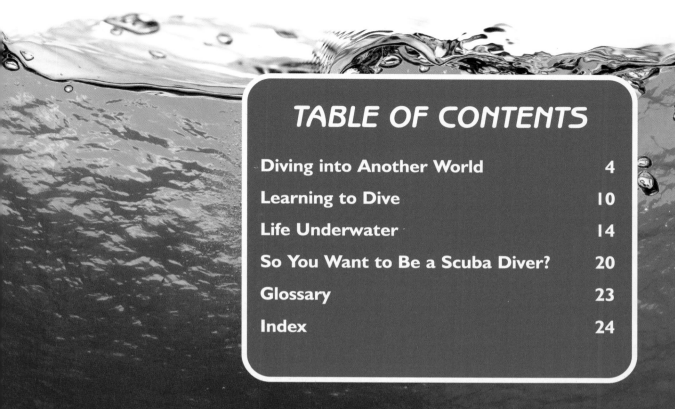

TABLE OF CONTENTS

DIVING INTO
ANOTHER WORLD

Scuba diving is like traveling to another world right here on planet Earth. No other outdoor sport lets a person experience a different world like scuba diving. It opens a fascinating underwater universe to the diver.

Like astronauts exploring the moon, scuba divers explore the underwater wonders of the sea.

Scuba stands for Self-Contained Underwater Breathing **Apparatus**. It allows divers to do something no human being can otherwise do: breathe underwater. Scuba divers can stay underwater for as long as their **compressed** air supply allows.

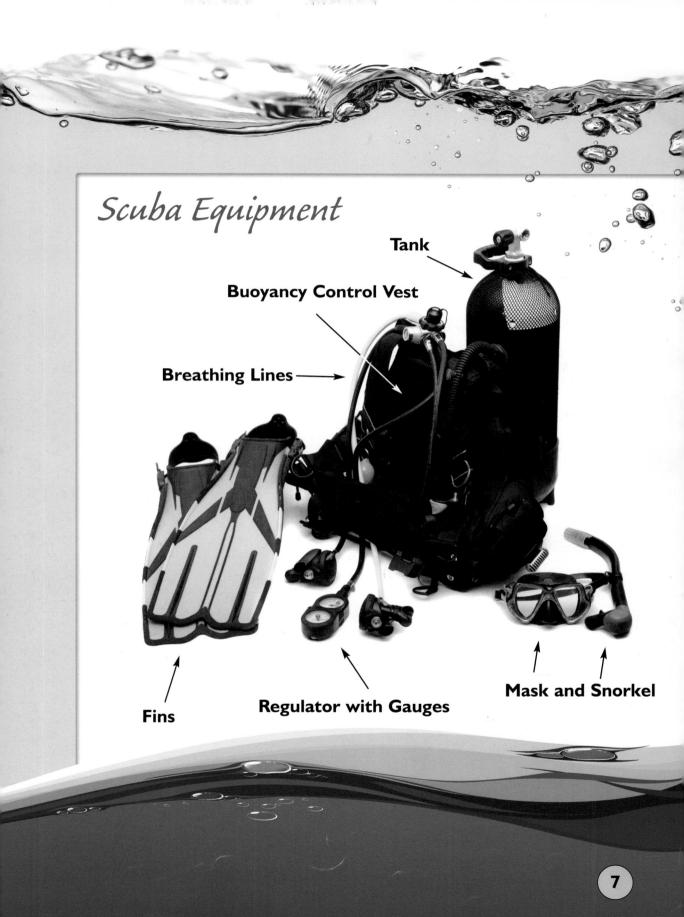

Scuba Equipment

Tank

Buoyancy Control Vest

Breathing Lines

Fins

Regulator with Gauges

Mask and Snorkel

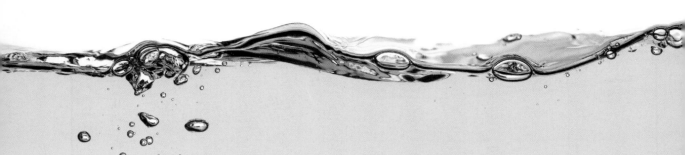

For as long as humans have entered water to swim, they have been limited in their ability to explore the underwater world. In the past century, various advances in **portable** underwater air supplies have led to modern scuba diving and made it much easier for humans to explore beneath the water's surface.

French inventor Jacques Cousteau is among the most important underwater explorers and scuba divers of all time.

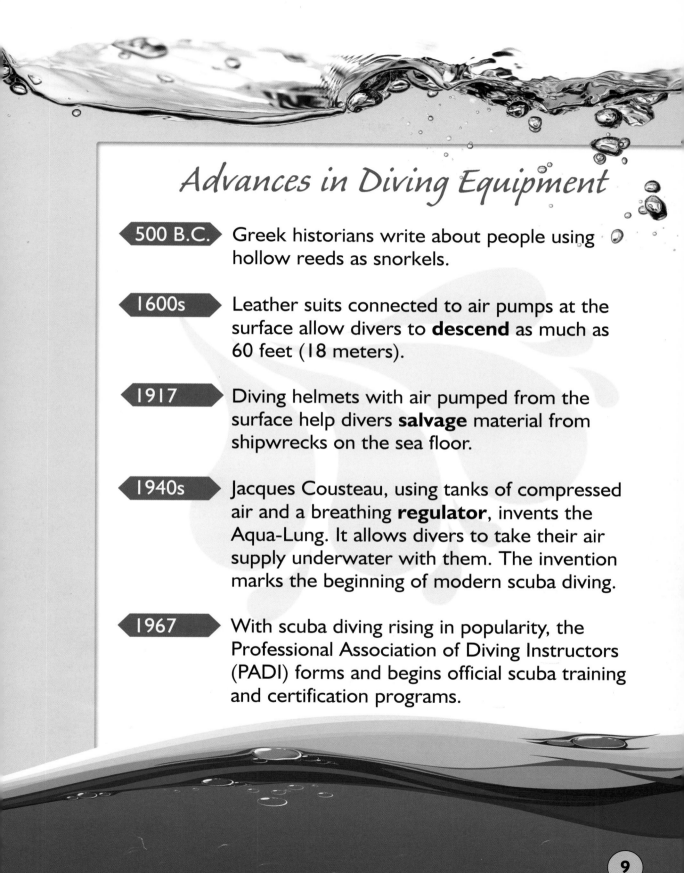

Advances in Diving Equipment

500 B.C. Greek historians write about people using hollow reeds as snorkels.

1600s Leather suits connected to air pumps at the surface allow divers to **descend** as much as 60 feet (18 meters).

1917 Diving helmets with air pumped from the surface help divers **salvage** material from shipwrecks on the sea floor.

1940s Jacques Cousteau, using tanks of compressed air and a breathing **regulator**, invents the Aqua-Lung. It allows divers to take their air supply underwater with them. The invention marks the beginning of modern scuba diving.

1967 With scuba diving rising in popularity, the Professional Association of Diving Instructors (PADI) forms and begins official scuba training and certification programs.

LEARNING TO DIVE

Before ever entering the water, people wanting to dive must take a course to learn how to function underwater using the necessary equipment. Passing this course means a person is certified to scuba dive.

Most PADI courses require students to be at least 10 years old to take an introductory course in a swimming pool.

Snorkeling is a good way for swimmers interested in diving to get comfortable seeing, moving, and breathing underwater.

Diving Discovery Fact

Snorkelers use a mask to see, and fins to move quickly. The **snorkel** allows breathing underwater. But, snorkelers must stay at or near the surface to breathe, while scuba divers have greater underwater freedom.

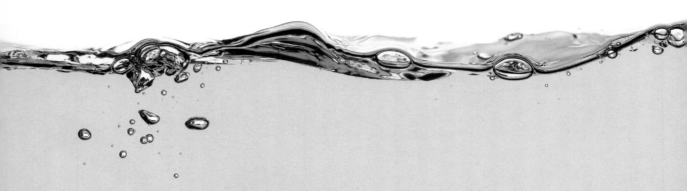

Like any sport, scuba diving requires repetition and practice in order to become comfortable. After all, breathing air underwater does not come naturally for human beings.

Scuba diving does bring an element of danger. As a result, scuba divers should never dive alone.

LIFE UNDERWATER

When divers enter the water, they first must remember to breathe! They adjust their **buoyancy** control by letting air into or out of their vests. For safety's sake, they must know how much air is in their tank so they can return to the surface before it runs out. Divers always have their own air line plus an **auxiliary** line in case another diver needs to share their air.

Diving Discovery Fact

A scuba diver carries at least a 40-pound (18-kilogram) tank of compressed air into the water. For young or small divers, that might seem heavy, but the equipment becomes almost weightless underwater.

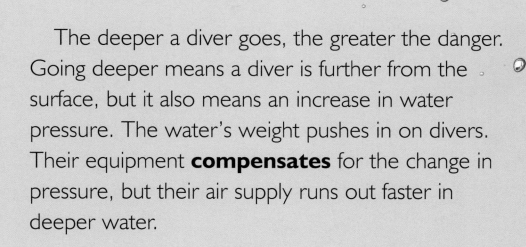

The deeper a diver goes, the greater the danger. Going deeper means a diver is further from the surface, but it also means an increase in water pressure. The water's weight pushes in on divers. Their equipment **compensates** for the change in pressure, but their air supply runs out faster in deeper water.

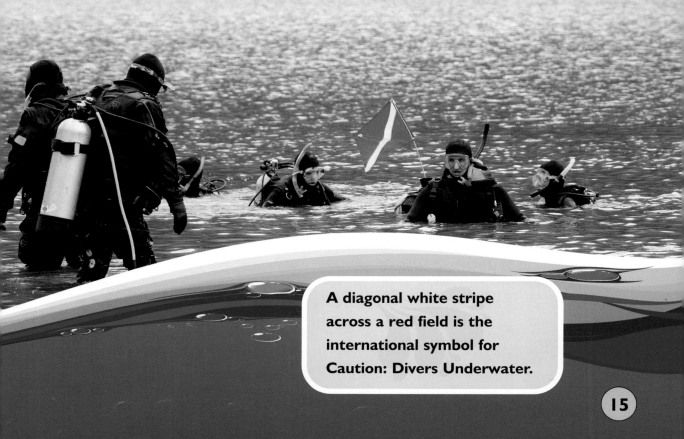

A diagonal white stripe across a red field is the international symbol for Caution: Divers Underwater.

Scuba divers head for some of the most **exotic** places on the planet. A **coral reef** provides excellent diving conditions. The water around reefs tends to be shallow and clear, giving divers a chance to see many underwater plants and animals. North America's Great Lakes are popular among divers who like to explore **shipwrecks**.

Diving Discovery Fact

The Great Barrier Reef, off Australia's east coast, may well be the king of all scuba diving sites. The waters surrounding this, the world's largest coral reef, are full of wild underwater plants and animals. Among them is the legendary great white shark.

More than a million and a half tourists flock to the Great Barrier Reef each year. Many of them are divers out to explore its underwater scenery.

Most people who dive are recreational divers. That means they do it for fun. Commercial divers do it as their job. They dive to perform underwater bridge construction or recover valuable things from underwater places.

Commercial divers sometimes work to bring a sunken ship's cargo to the surface for recovery.

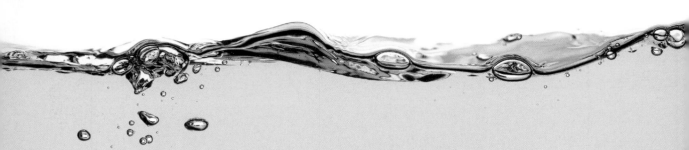

SO YOU WANT TO BE A SCUBA DIVER?

If you enjoy swimming and wish you could breathe underwater, scuba diving lets you do just that. Divers leave the gravity of life on land and enter a weightless, **alien** world of underwater life forms and scenery.

Diving Discovery Fact

Scuba diving has become popular. More than 900,000 people become PADI certified in scuba diving each year.

How low can they go? Scuba divers can go about 130 feet (40 meters) underwater before the water pressure becomes too dangerous.

If you enjoy exploring new places and out-of-this-world experiences, then sign up for a scuba diving class. You'll soon witness the wonders of life underwater.

Glossary

alien (AY-lee-uhn): different, strange, or foreign

apparatus (ap-uh-RAT-uhss): equipment or machine used to do a job

auxiliary (awg-ZIL-yur-ee): extra support or help

buoyancy (BOI-uhn-see): the ability to float without sinking

compensates (KOM-puhn-sates): makes up for something by design

compressed (kuhm-PRESST): squeezed in order to fit into a small space

coral (KOR-uhl): a hard, underwater substance made of the skeletons of millions of sea creatures

descend (di-SEND): to go down to a lower level

exotic (eg-ZOT-ik): strange, fascinating

portable (POR-tuh-buhl): able to be moved or carried with ease

reef (REEF): a strip of rock or coral close to the surface of a lake or ocean

regulator (REG-yuh-late-uhr): a device which controls or manages breathable air

salvage (SAL-vij): to rescue property from a sunken ship

shipwrecks (SHIP-reks): the remains of sunken ships at the bottom of oceans, lakes, or rivers

snorkel (SNOR-kuhl): a tube you can use to breathe through while swimming underwater

Index

Websites

www.padi.com/scuba/default.aspx

www.divingcairns.com.au/diving.html

www.greatlakesunderwater.com/greatlakesdiving.html

marinebio.org/Oceans/S_C_U_B_A

About the Author

Tom Greve lives in Chicago with his wife, Meg, and their children, Madison and William. He enjoys playing, watching, and writing about sports of all kinds.